EVERYDAY INSIGHTS

Wisdom in your pocket

Liza G. Espinosa

PRESS

Everyday Insights
Wisdom in your pocket
by Liza G. Espinosa

Printed in the United States of America

ISBN 9781498424134

www.xulonpress.com

DEDICATION

To my parents Milagros and Leonardo Espinosa, my brother Leo, Melody (my precious treasure), Ate Angie and my late grandmother Benita – who made home a good place to learn.

ACKNOWLEDGMENTS

The following have given me insights:

Frecy Hough for the idea of quotation and bible verse.

Yomi Olawale for the backcover concept.

Jason Pelplinski for his teaching "What's In Your Hand?"

Pastor Mick Shah for his Sunday sermon "What's In your Hand?"

Kathy Ermino for her encouragement and technical help.

Pastors Ogie and Elena Ramos for being my spiritual parents.

Janet Bailey for showing me the value of staying in God's presence.

Pamela Bailey for always reminding me that life is full of possibilities.

Fatima Arador for her motherly advice and prayers.

Ruth Gordon for encouraging me to take the last steps to finish this book.

Doctors and nurses that I have worked with over the years.

EVERYDAY INSIGHTS

1) When you see God in everything, He gives color to everything.

"The thief comes only in order to steal, kill and destroy. I have come in order that you might have life —- life in all its fullness," (John 10:10 GNB).

2) Dwelling in God's love is enough to get you through in life.

"The Lord your God is with you. He is mighty to save. He will take great delight in you. He will quiet you with His love. He will rejoice over you with singing," (Zeph. 3:17 NIV).

3) God blesses our abilities, but there is one ability that brings a far greater blessing – the ability to depend on Him.

"My soul, wait silently for God alone. For my expectation is from Him. He only is my rock and my salvation. He is my defense. I shall not be moved," (Ps. 62:5-6 NKJV).

4) The good thing about our God is that if you make a mistake the first time, there is still hope. In heavenly terms, this is called GRACE.

"And God is able to make all grace abound toward you, that you, always having all sufficiency in all things, may have an abundance for every good work" (2 Cor. 9:8 NKJV).

5) When God closes the door, He opens the windows and the roof.

"Now to Him who is able to do exceedingly abundantly above all that we ask or think, according to the power that works in us. To Him be glory in the church by Christ Jesus to all generations, forever and ever Amen," (Eph. 3:20,21 NKJV).

6) There is really no secret to being anointed. It is just staying in the presence of God.

"You will show me the path of life. In your presence is fullness of joy. At your right hand are pleasures forevermore," (Ps. 16:11 NKJV).

7) I will never be convinced that you know God, if you cannot wait for His timing.

"To everything there is a season. A time for every purpose under heaven," (Eccles. 3:1 NKJV).

8) No matter how long winter seems to be, summer will surely come. .

"For the vision is yet for an appointed time but at the end it will speak, and it will not lie. Though it tarries, wait for it because it will surely come. It will not tarry," (Hab. 2:3 NKJV).

9) The truth will not only stand the test of time and set you free; it will help you face reality.

"As the Lord's servant, you must not quarrel. You must be kind towards all, a good and patient teacher, gentle as you correct your opponents, for it may be that God will give them the opportunity to repent and come to know the truth," (2 Tim. 2:24 GNB).

10) Change can be scary, uncomfortable and unpopular, but I can face the unknown because God knows what I do not know. Take delight in what God is doing in your life.

"Call to me, and I will answer you; I will tell you wonderful and marvelous things that you know nothing about," (Jer. 33:3 GNB).

11) Silence is golden. It brings a far greater conviction to others than any strategic approach to wake up a person's conscience.

"In the multitude of words, sin is not lacking. But he who restrains his lips is wise," (Prov. 10:19 NKJV).

12) Our reactions matter a lot when correction comes: Either you accept the truth and start all over again, or you put up your pride and make it worse.

"If you refuse to learn, you are hurting yourself. If you accept correction, you will become wiser," (Prov. 15:32 GNB).

13) I do not need to learn a lot of lessons in one mistake, because one mistake is already a big lesson. That, in itself, is enough for me to be careful the next time around.

"For a righteous man may fall seven times and rise again. But the wicked shall fall by calamity," (Prov. 24:16 NKJV).

14) Sometimes it only takes one occasion to show your love and start a life, or journey, with a person. It can also take one occasion to be careless and lose the person entirely.

"Be very careful then how you live —- not as unwise but as wise, making the most of every opportunity because the days are evil," (Eph. 5:15 NIV).

15) A little light can make a difference, if you let it shine.

"You yourselves used to be in the darkness, but since you have become the Lord's people, you are in the light. So you must live like people who belong to the light, for it is the light that brings a rich harvest of every kind of goodness, righteousness, and truth," (Eph.5:8-9 GNB) .

16) The condition of our pockets should not change the condition of our relationship with God.

" For the love of money is a root of all kinds of evil, for which some have strayed from the faith in their greediness, and pierced themselves through with many sorrow," (1 Tim.6:10 NKJV).

17) When we are hurting, it is good to be on bended knees. This act allows us to talk to God about the person, rather than talk to others about the person.

"Whoever guards his mouth and tongue keeps his soul from troubles," (Prov. 21:23 NKJV).

18) An amazing attribute of God is...He never grows old. That means forgetfulness has no place in His heart. He always does what He promised; He is ageless. In fact, He is called the "Ancient of Days".

"For no matter how many promises God has made, they are 'Yes' in Christ. And so through Him the "Amen" is spoken by us to the glory of God," (2 Cor.1:20 NIV).

19) Dwelling in the past is like driving a car, where your foot is always pressing on the brakes. You cannot move forward, and you may not ever reach your destination.

"Brethren, I do not count myself to have apprehended; but one thing I do, forgetting those things which are behind and reaching forward to those things which are ahead, I press toward the goal for the prize of the upward call of God in Christ Jesus," (Phil. 3:13,14 NKJV).

20) Tell me how many days you work in a week, how much time you spend with God, and I will tell you how strong or weak you will be in times of temptation.

"Keep watch and pray that you will not fall into temptation. The spirit is willing, but the flesh is weak," (Matt. 26:41 GNB).

21) You do not have to struggle to sing better. You just need to have a song in your heart.

"Therefore do not be unwise, but understand what the will of the Lord is. And do not be drunk with wine, in which is dissipation; but be filled with the Spirit, speaking to one another in psalms and hymns and spiritual songs, singing and making melody in your heart to the Lord," (Eph. 5:17-19 NKJV).

22) Everyday, when we wake up, we experience the miracle of opening our eyes and knowing that we are alive. Thank God for the gift of life.

"Grace and peace be multiplied to you in the knowledge of God and of Jesus our Lord, as His divine power has given to us all things that pertain to life and godliness, through the knowledge of Him who called us by glory and virtue," (2 Pet. 1:2-4 NKJV).

23) We do not hold time, but we can hold a part of it... It is called "TODAY".

"But do not forget this one thing, dear friends: With the Lord a day is like a thousand years, and a thousand years are like a day," (2 Pet. 3:8 NIV).

24) The words "I am sorry" are miracle-working words. They are better than any surgical method in closing wounds.

"He has shown you, O man, what is good and what does the Lord require of you but to do justly and to love mercy and to walk humbly with your God," (Mic. 6:8 NKJV)

25) God is interested in the influence we have in the work-place. He knows and appreciates every effort, and never forgets about them.

"So then, my dear brothers and sisters, stand firm and steady. Keep busy always in your work for the Lord, since you know that nothing you do in the Lord's service is ever useless." (1 Cor. 15:58 GNB)

26) Have a song in your heart, and your voice will follow.

"He has put a new song in my mouth. Praise to our God. Many will see it and fear and will trust in the Lord," (Ps. 40:3 NKJV).

27) Let God surprise you as He fills the pages of your life.

"The Lord repay your work, and a full reward be given you by the Lord God of Israel, under whose wings you have come for refuge," (Ruth 2:12 NKJV).

28) Pursue excellence by walking in the precepts of God.

"Do your best to win full approval in God's sight, as a worker who is not ashamed of his work, one who correctly teaches the message of God's truth," (2 Tim. 2:15 GNB).

29) God knows already who can make us smile today.

"You saw me before I was born. The days allotted to me had all been recorded in your book before any of them ever began," (Ps. 139:16 GNB).

30) Honesty is measured by a series of truths.

"The Lord abhors dishonest scales, but accurate weights are His delight," (Prov. 11:1 NIV).

31) If your walk with God is deep, why have shallow choices in life?

"There is a way that seems right to a man, but in the end it leads to death," (Prov. 14:12 NIV).

32) It is always a blessing to have somebody that will remind you to think of the goodness of Jesus Christ.

"I thank my God upon every remembrance of you, always in every prayer of mine, making request for you all with joy for your fellowship in the gospel from the first day until now, being confident of this very thing, that He who has begun a good work in you will complete it until the day of Jesus Christ," (Phil. 1:3-5 NKJV).

33) Giving false compliments just to make a person feel good is tantamount to telling lies in a nice way.

"A lying tongue hates those it hurts and a flattering mouth works ruin," (Prov. 26: 28 NIV).

34) Life is simple; it only becomes complicated when you deviate from the truth.

"Sincerity and truth are what you require. Fill my mind with your wisdom," (Ps. 51:6 GNB).

35) Encouraging words can enable somebody to live another day.

"A word fitly spoken is like apples of gold in settings of silver," (Prov. 25:11 NKJV).

36) God can bring us exactly where He wants us to be. He can arrange every detail: He plans the journey and makes it happen. Everything will turn out exactly as it is meant to be.

"For I know the thoughts that I think toward you, says the Lord, thoughts of peace and not of evil, to give you a future and a hope," (Jer. 29:11 NKJV).

37) People expect to be blessed, and yet they go on hating somebody; just a reminder that blessing and hatred do not go together.

"Make sure that there is no one here today who hears these solemn demands and yet convinces himself that all will be well with him, even if he stubbornly goes his own way. That would destroy all of you, good and evil alike," (Deut. 29:19 GNB).

38) What you believe is what you get.

"So Jesus answered and said to them, 'Have faith in God. For assuredly, I say to you, whoever says to this mountain, 'Be removed and be cast into the sea,' and does not doubt in his heart, but believes that those things he says will be done, he will have whatever he says,'" (Mark 11:22-23 NKJV).

39) God's favor is not just for a season: it is for a lifetime.

"Surely goodness and love will follow me all the days of my life, and I will dwell in the house of the Lord for ever," (Ps. 23:6 NIV).

40) God is good; therefore, in whatever point we are in our lives, it is good. God is good; therefore life is great. Value each day; take time to laugh. There will always be funny things to laugh at, and people to laugh with. Enjoy life today.

"Nehemiah said, 'Go and enjoy choice food and sweet drinks and send some to those who have nothing prepared. This day is sacred to our Lord. Do not grieve, for the joy of the Lord is your strength,'" (Neh. 8:10 NIV).

41) We can be at peace, if at times we do not get exactly what we want, because it is only God who can define what is GOOD for us.

"How wonderful are the good things you keep for those who honor you! Everyone knows how good you are, how securely you protect those who trust you," (Ps. 31:19 GNB).

42) You can tell a person's relationship with God by the decisions they make. They make choices that lead to life.

"I call heaven and earth as witnesses today against you, that I have set before you life and death, blessing and cursing; therefore choose life, that both you and your descendants may live, that you may love the Lord your God, that you may obey His voice, and that you may cling to Him, for He is your life and the length of your days; and that you may dwell in the land which the Lord swore to your fathers, to Abraham, Isaac, and Jacob, to give them," (Deut. 30:19-20 NKJV).

43) Being mentored by a person who has a heart for God is like traveling in the train. It will keep you from being derailed.

"And this is my prayer: that your love may abound more and more in knowledge and depth of insight, so that you may be able to discern what is best and may be pure and blameless until the day of Christ, filled with the fruit of righteousness that comes through Jesus Christ —- to the glory and praise of God," (Phil. 1:9-11 NIV).

44) Compliance leads to wellness.

"Obey the Lord, and you will live longer. The wicked die before their time," (Prov. 10:27 GNB).

45) A life of surrender is not deprivation. In fact, it opens to new doors of hope for bringing about change.

"So then, my brothers and sisters, because of God's mercy to us I appeal to you: offer yourselves as a living sacrifice to God, dedicated to His service and pleasing to Him. This is the true worship that you should offer. Do not conform yourselves to the standards of this world, but let God transform you inwardly by a complete change of your mind. Then you will be able to know the will of God – what is good and is pleasing to him and is perfect," (Rom. 12:1-2 GNB).

46 The place of sacrifice can be the very place of blessing.

"An altar of earth you shall make for Me, and you shall sacrifice on it your burnt offerings and your peace offerings, your sheep and your oxen. In every place where I record My name I will come to you, and I will bless you," (Exod. 20:24 NKJV).

47) Good character attracts good company.

"Keep company with the wise and you will become wise. If you make friends with stupid people, you will be ruined," (Prov. 13:20 GNB).

48) Being successful is being with the right people: they will encourage you and lift you up to keep you going: they will show you which road to take to keep you on track. Lastly, they may correct you for you to have the right attitude in your daily endeavor.

"Where there is no counsel, the people fall; But in the multitude of counselors there is safety," (Prov. 11:14 NKJV).

49) Along your journey in life, you will need the counsel of your parents somehow, somewhere, sometime.

"My son, hear the instruction of your father and do not forsake the law of your mother, for they will be a graceful ornament on your head and chains about your neck," (Prov. 1:8-9 NKJV).

50) In fulfilling a dream, it is the first steps that unravel the impediments in pursuing its realization. Take the first step; then it will lead you to the next.

"The steps of a good man are ordered by the Lord and He delights in his way. Though he fall, he shall not be utterly cast down. For the Lord upholds him with His hand," (Ps. 37:23-24 NKJV).